Can I tell you about Eating Disorders?

Can I tell you about...?

The "Can I tell you about...?" series offers simple introductions to a range of limiting conditions and other issues that affect our lives. Friendly characters invite readers to learn about their experiences, the challenges they face and how they would like to be helped and supported. These books serve as excellent starting points for family and classroom discussions.

Other subjects covered in the "Can I tell you about...?" series

ADHD

Adoption

Anxiety

Autism

Asperger Syndrome

Asthma

Cerebral Palsy

Dementia

Diabetes (Type 1)

Dyslexia

Dyspraxia

Epilepsy

ME/Chronic Fatigue Syndrome

OCD

Parkinson's Disease

Selective Mutism

Stammering/Stuttering

Stroke

Tourette Syndrome

Can I tell you about Eating Disorders?

A guide for friends, family and professionals

BRYAN LASK AND LUCY WATSON
Illustrated by Fiona Field

Jessica Kingsley *Publishers*
London and Philadelphia

First published in 2014
by Jessica Kingsley Publishers
73 Collier Street
London N1 9BE, UK
and
400 Market Street, Suite 400
Philadelphia, PA 19106, USA

www.jkp.com

Copyright © Bryan Lask and Lucy Watson 2014
Illustrations copyright © Fiona Field 2014

Library of Congress Cataloging in Publication Data
A CIP catalog record for this book is available from the Library of Congress

British Library Cataloguing in Publication Data
A CIP catalogue record for this book is available from the British Library

ISBN 978 1 84905 421 8
eISBN 978 0 85700 797 1

Printed and bound in Great Britain by Bell and Bain Ltd, Glasgow

Lucy dedicates this, her first book, to Mum and Dad, Ed and Pops for no matter how many fights are had, family is where life starts and love never ends.

Bryan dedicates this book to all the children with eating problems whom he has treated and who have taught him so much.

Acknowledgements

Many thanks go to Fiona Field for her wonderful illustrations; and to our colleagues at JKP for giving us the opportunity to write this book, but to Lucy Buckroyd in particular for being so patient and understanding!

Contents

Introduction

This book has been written for boys and girls aged about 7–15 years old to help them to understand and learn about the different eating disorders. It tells them what types of eating disorders there are, what it feels like to have them and how they can help.

"There are many different types of eating disorders. I've got one type called Anorexia Nervosa but let me introduce my friends Beth, Freddie, Sam and Francesca who have other types..."

Hello.
My name is Francesca.
I have Functional Dysphagia,
and I can't eat solid food
because I think I'm going
to choke or vomit!

"So you see, we all have different eating disorders and we want to tell you about them, what it feels like to have them, and how you might help us deal with them – if you want to."

"We all act and look like everybody else...apart from Alice and Freddie. People with Anorexia Nervosa and Food Avoidance Emotional Disorder are easier to notice than the rest of us; they eat very little so they become very thin."

Alice: "You can't see that we have eating disorders. On the outside we look like everybody else."

Sam: "Except for you, Alice, and Freddie. Everybody can tell that you have eating disorders because you don't eat and you are really skinny."

Alice: "Don't be silly, Sam! I'm fatter than all of you!"

Sam: "Isn't that the problem with Anorexia Nervosa? It makes you feel fat when actually you're thin."

Alice: "Anyway, as I was saying, you wouldn't be able to tell we have our eating disorders straightaway as we act like everybody else."

Beth: "We love to do things just like what other children our age do. We like swimming, tennis, running, reading, drawing, playing games...all sorts."

Francesca: "The main way you might be able to spot we have eating disorders is if you see us around food."

All: "EURGH...food!"

"It is not because we simply don't like certain types of food. We all have different reasons for avoiding food which we will try to explain."

Alice: "Most people don't realise it, but they may naturally avoid certain types of food. Most children love sweets, cakes and other sweet things; but don't like eating celery, Brussels sprouts or other sour things. If you don't like a food because of its smell, taste or what it looks like, then you would naturally try to avoid it (even when your mum tells you just to try a tiny bit!).

People with all types of eating disorders avoid food too. But it's not that they don't like certain foods. Their eating disorders control *which* foods, what *types* of foods and *how much* food they avoid. That's something that people find quite hard to understand.

You might notice that sometimes people with eating disorders won't eat *any* food (like Freddie and me), or they may *look* like they eat normally (like Beth), or they may only eat certain *types* of food (like Sam and Francesca).

Over the next few pages we will try and explain why each of us avoids food."

"I think I'm fat, even though people tell me I'm thin. I feel so full, even though I haven't eaten anything. Losing weight is what I need to do, even though many people tell me that it's dangerous and I need to put on weight."

Alice: "Let's start with me. I have Anorexia Nervosa, which is probably the eating disorder you have heard of, or will hear about, the most. I try to avoid eating any food whenever I can. When it is impossible to avoid food though (like when my mum or my teacher is watching me when it's a mealtime) I just try and eat the smallest amount of food I can!

Sometimes I'm hungry but I can't bear to eat because I think I'm fat. I think I am the fattest person on earth, so I try not to eat anything at all because I want to lose weight so badly! I am so so SO scared that if I eat anything at all I will put on weight and get even fatter."

Sam: "Alice, I don't understand why you can't see what we can all see. You are so skinny – you eat so little and exercise so much that you really are far skinnier than anyone else!"

Alice: "That's the problem with having Anorexia Nervosa, Sam. No matter what anyone tells me, I truly believe I am fat, ugly, greedy and hopeless. I believe that if I eat I will get even fatter, even if that may seem ridiculous to everyone else."

"Sometimes I lose control and eat and eat
and eat. Then, later on I feel disgusting
so I decide to exercise, be sick or not eat
again. Unlike Alice and Freddie, I don't
look like I have an eating disorder – I am
a normal weight so don't look skinny."

Beth: "Sometimes I feel like Alice but in a slightly different way. I have Bulimia Nervosa, which may be another eating disorder you have heard of. Unlike Alice, sometimes I can't stop myself from eating. I seem to lose all control and end up eating so much food all in one go. This is called a *binge*. When I binge, I can eat three or four times as much food as you would normally eat in one meal!

Like Alice though, after I finish my binge, I feel fat, gross and ugly. To make myself feel better I sometimes have to get rid of the food I have just eaten by making myself sick. This is called a *purge*."

Sam: "Ewww – gross!"

Beth: "I know – I feel gross about myself. Sometimes though I just decide not to eat (like Alice and Freddie) for a very long time or go and exercise lots. You probably wouldn't know I have an eating disorder if you looked at me – I am a normal weight, not skinny like Alice and Freddie."

"People with Food Avoidance Emotional Disorder look like people with Anorexia Nervosa (like Alice), but people with Food Avoidance Emotional Disorder do not worry about their weight or shape...they are just very anxious and sad, so they don't feel hungry and don't eat."

Freddie: "Unlike Beth, lots of people may look at me and think I am like Alice – they think I have Anorexia Nervosa because I am very skinny and I avoid food. But my eating disorder is called Food Avoidance Emotional Disorder."

Sam: "Food...Avoidance...Emotional...Disorder... could they not come up with something shorter?"

Freddie: "Ha ha. What it means is that I get very anxious, like all of us here, and most of the time feel very sad too and just can't face eating food – I just don't have an appetite. I don't have any problems with my weight or shape, unlike Alice and Beth, but my worry and low mood (feeling sad) are SO BIG that I don't eat...and that's why I'm so skinny."

"I can only eat these things. Anything else you
make me try and eat will make me feel sick.
So if you invite me round for a meal you will
have to make sure you have these things –
and the right brands of them – at home."

Sam: "Unlike Alice and Freddie who you can tell are very skinny, if you saw me at school, at the shops or in the street you wouldn't be able to tell that I had an eating disorder (so I'm like Beth!). But if you invited me round to your house for a meal – then you would be able to tell that there is something different about my eating. My eating disorder is quite common: I have Selective Eating. Unlike Alice I don't think I'm fat."

Alice: "Well, if you don't think you're fat then why do you avoid food?"

Sam: "Freddie doesn't think he's fat and he avoids food too! The difference between Freddie and me is that Freddie gets so worried and sad he can't eat. But I'm different because I *can* eat, but I only eat a few types of food and nothing else."

Alice: "So what food can you eat?"

Sam: "I can only eat: chips, bananas, cream crackers, Marmite sandwiches and baked beans. I can only drink water or strawberry milkshakes too. I'm also very picky about which brands I like! If you tried to give me anything else, even just looking at it would disgust me. If I *had* to eat it, I would feel sick – and that's why it would be hard if I came round for a meal!"

"If you looked at me you wouldn't know I had an eating disorder but around lumpy and solid food I become so scared. I can't eat it because I think if I do it will make me sick or choke!"

Alice: "You've been very quiet, Francesca. Why do you avoid food?"

Francesca: "Well I have an eating disorder that's a bit different from all of you. My eating disorder is called Functional Dysphagia."

Sam: "Dys-what-e-yer?"

Francesca: "It means that I have a fear of swallowing food, especially lumpy or solid foods – I have to avoid those! Like Sam and Freddie, I don't think I'm fat, but I do think if I put lumpy or solid food in my mouth I'm going to choke or be sick."

Freddie: "So, are you like me – do you worry so much that you can't eat?"

Francesca: "No, Freddie, but I understand why you would think that. I am not as generally worried and low in mood as you, but I do get very worried about solid and lumpy foods because I think if I eat them, I will choke or be sick."

Alice: "So you see, we all avoid food but we avoid it for different reasons. We will now try to explain these different reasons on the next few pages."

"People with Anorexia Nervosa think they're fat. They also think they are failures when they are actually successful. They feel shame, guilt and disgust with themselves. They want to be perfect and are never happy with what they achieve."

Alice: "Eating disorders are much more than problems with eating. Lots of people don't know that because of the name 'eating disorder'. Take Freddie, for example – he can be so worried (sometimes called anxious) and sad about things that he can't eat. I'm a bit like Freddie because I get very anxious too. But my anxiety is all about getting fat. Anorexia Nervosa also controls the way I feel about myself: it makes me have low self-esteem. That means I don't have much confidence in myself and often I think I'm a failure."

Sam: "But you're top of the class – you're *not* a failure and you've been very confident taking charge of this book."

Alice: "The thing is, Sam, I set myself very high standards and I work hard to achieve them. Some people say I'm a perfectionist, which means I have to get things absolutely perfect. Sometimes I will re-do work over and over again until it's absolutely right, but the thing is I *never* think it's right."

Sam: "Is that why you exercise all the time too – to get what you think is the perfect body?"

Alice: "Yes. Other people will tell you I have something called distorted body image, which means that I might not see my body and shape in the same way that you see it. I think I'm fat and disgusting in every way. But also sometimes I can't stop myself from moving no matter how many times I'm told to stop."

"People with Bulimia Nervosa think
they are failures; they feel shame and
disgust, and hate themselves. They may
also often react without thinking."

"People with Selective Eating may find new things and changes to their routine difficult."

"People with Food Avoidance Emotional
Disorder have low mood, feel worried
and have no appetite."

Beth: "Although Alice doesn't eat and I do (sometimes), we share the same lack of confidence (what she called low self-esteem). Because of my Bulimia Nervosa, I feel very guilty and disgusted with myself when I binge on lots of food. Alice and I are both very unhappy with our weight and shape. Our eating disorders try to tell us all the time that we are bad and should not be happy with the way we are. They make us hate ourselves.

I am different from Alice though as I am loud, outgoing, bubbly and sometimes I act impulsively. That means that sometimes I don't think about what I am about to do, I just act quickly and do it."

Sam: "I don't have the same problems as Alice and Beth. With my Selective Eating, apart from food, the only thing that worries me is that sometimes I do not like new people or places, and sometimes I find it hard to wear new clothes. I like sticking to my routine and what I know – just like the food I know I can eat. And like Alice and Freddie I often feel very anxious."

Freddie: "Yes, Sam, my Food Avoidance Emotional Disorder makes me worry so much and often makes me feel so sad that I just can't eat, no matter what others tell me to do. I never feel hungry."

"Not everyone has to have such a horrible experience to 'get' Functional Dysphagia. Sometimes they will just believe that some food will make them sick and others will believe the food will choke them."

Francesca: "My eating disorder controls me in different ways. My Functional Dysphagia tells me that I am going to choke or be sick if I eat certain types of food. But it doesn't make me think I'm fat or disgusting, and I'm actually quite confident."

Alice: "So, if you don't think you're fat, then what do you think caused your Functional Dysphagia?"

Francesca: "Well, not everyone who has Functional Dysphagia 'gets it' in the same way. I think what caused mine was when I was little, my Granny came for Sunday lunch and she choked on a chicken bone and I was so scared. I was so terrified that ever since then I haven't been able to eat anything that's solid because I'm afraid it's going to happen to me!"

Alice: "What, *just* from seeing your Grandma...?"

Francesca: "Yes! Ever since then I've been feeling so worried that I can only eat mushed-up or soft foods, like porridge – but it cannot have lumps. Yes, yes, I know...it doesn't make sense!"

All: "That's the thing about eating disorders, they *just don't make sense!*"

"Unlike other people, those people with Selective Eating do not seem to have grown out of their fussy eating behaviour from when they were little."

Alice: "What about you, Sam – what do you think causes Selective Eating?"

Sam: "Well, when I was younger I was a bit fussy – most children are when they are little. The thing is, that normally children stop being so fussy when they grow older and start eating more and different types of food. Selective Eaters like me just don't seem to grow out of it. Like me, they carry on only eating the small range of foods they always have done.

What about you and Beth? What do you think causes your Anorexia Nervosa and Bulimia Nervosa?"

Alice: "That is a very difficult question to answer, Sam. It is one of the questions so many people ask, but unfortunately the doctors and professors out there don't have a definite answer for us yet."

Beth: "Anorexia and Bulimia Nervosa do not have one single thing that causes them. There are many different things that can combine to create each of these two eating disorders."

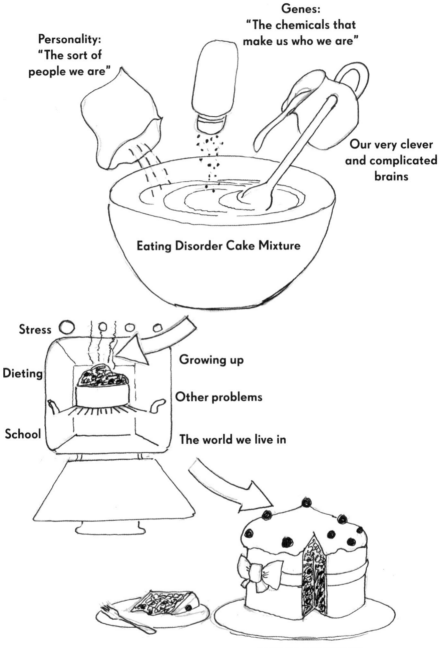

Personality:
"The sort of
people we are"

Genes:
"The chemicals that
make us who we are"

Our very clever
and complicated
brains

Eating Disorder Cake Mixture

Stress

Dieting

School

Growing up

Other problems

The world we live in

EATING DISORDER

Alice: "There are lots of people out there who are trying to work out what causes Anorexia and Bulimia Nervosa. The problem is that there are *lots* of causes and they will almost always mix together."

Beth: "It's a bit like making a cake. You know you need the ingredients. You know you need the mixture or recipe. Only then will you be able to work out how to make the cake."

Alice: "So, the wacky professors know that there are lots of ingredients that can be used to make the Anorexia or Bulimia Nervosa cake. The problem is that they haven't actually worked out the exact recipe."

Beth: "AND one person with Anorexia or Bulimia Nervosa may have a completely different recipe and different set of ingredients from another person with the same eating disorder."

All: "It's confusing! And you know? It's OK to be confused!"

Alice: "The picture on the opposite page might help. But don't worry, there are lots of nerdy doctors and professors out there still trying to work it out."

"It's really hard at school. People stare,
ask questions, and whisper about us.
They just don't seem to understand."

Alice: "One of the hardest things about having Anorexia Nervosa is going to school. I don't like it when people stare at me – it makes me feel worse about myself. When I don't have anything to eat my friends don't understand why and keep offering me food and telling me I should eat it. Because of this, I try to go and sit somewhere else other than the dining hall at lunchtime. Most of the time I go to the library to get on with my homework."

Sam: "What about me? Every day my friends laugh at me because my Selective Eating means I only eat certain foods. They offer me things from their lunchboxes and say I should try them. They don't seem to understand that new foods disgust me and often make me feel sick."

Francesca: "That's sort of like me. People don't realise that having Functional Dysphagia means the only foods I can have are soft, mushed-up foods that my mum makes for my lunch – like mashed potato but with *no* lumps. People laugh and say I'm eating baby food."

Freddie: "Me too! I know how hard it is for people to understand my Food Avoidance Emotional Disorder. But please try for a second to think how I feel: I am worried and feel sad all of the time and can't explain to others why I feel like that. I am SO worried and have such a low mood that I just can't eat. I can't explain it, and my brother and sister find it so annoying, but I just can't bring myself to eat any food."

"It can be really hard at home too."

Beth: "When I have a bad day at school it's going home that I find the hardest. At home there's an endless supply of food. There's food everywhere! And when I've had a bad day I start feeling like I'm losing control and that's when my Bulimia Nervosa takes over and I start to binge.

When I binge at home I can eat and eat and eat. There's food in the fridge, the freezer, the cupboards and baking tins. I really lose control and feel like I can't stop."

Sam: "That's what I like about home though – there's always food there I can eat. My Mum and Dad know which foods I can eat and which brands I like. At school my friends and teachers don't understand that."

Francesca: "But don't your mum and dad get annoyed sometimes? Mine do – my brother and sister get annoyed that I can only have non-lumpy foods."

Freddie: "I try to explain to my two sisters that I am so worried and sad that I can't bring myself to eat but they just get annoyed and don't understand. I do try not to be worried and sad, but it's a lot easier to say that than do it. I know that me being sad all the time might annoy my sisters, but I would love them to understand the way I feel."

"It's really hard on our families to deal with our eating disorders. We feel so bad about upsetting them and making them angry. But we can't help it. Our eating disorders control our behaviour. We want our families to understand."

Beth: "I feel really bad about my behaviour at home. I know that my parents get annoyed when I binge on so much food. It costs them a lot of money and I know they talk about it – I hear them arguing sometimes. I feel bad for my sister too. One time I lost control so badly that I ate her whole birthday cake the night before her birthday. And to make matters worse I then made myself sick."

Alice: "I cannot believe you ate your sister's birthday cake...and THEN made yourself be sick! No wonder your sister got cross. My brother gets cross at me too. Every time we have our family dinner he gets really angry when I don't eat the meal Mum or Dad has prepared. He says I'm selfish, that I'm just doing it to hurt them. He doesn't understand that I just can't eat.

Sam: "My parents also get cross with me. Like you Beth, I hear them talking about how my specific foods cost so much money because I have to have certain brands of foods. I feel so guilty, but I can't eat anything else other than a certain type of baked beans for example."

Alice: "There are a number of ways you can help me with my Anorexia Nervosa:

- Please don't expect me to understand what's happening inside me.

- Please try to understand that:

    - I get very worried about myself all the time.

    - I do not like myself.

    - I am full of shame, I am truly embarrassed by myself.

    - I feel guilty when I eat.

    - I know what I think about myself might seem silly to you, but I just can't help it!

- Please try to stay friends with me.

- Please try to remember that I like doing lots of things that you do.

- Please try to remember that I haven't chosen to be like this.

- You can help me best by treating me like any other person."

Beth: "There are a number of ways you can help me with my Bulimia Nervosa:

- It would be helpful if you could try to distract me after I've eaten.

- Please don't expect me to understand why I can't stop binging.

- Please try to remember after I've binged or purged that I feel full of shame.

Like Alice:

- Please try to stay friends with me.

- Please try to remember that I like doing lots of things that you do.

- Please try to remember that I haven't chosen to be like this.

- You can help me best by treating me like any other person."

Freddie: "There are a number of ways you can help me with my Food Avoidance Emotional Disorder:

- Please don't expect me to understand what's happening inside me.

- Please try to understand that I often feel sad and worried.

- I know what I think might seem silly to you, but please try to remember that I just can't help it.

Like Alice and Beth:

- Please try to stay friends with me.

- Please try to remember that I like doing lots of things that you do.

- Please try to remember that I haven't chosen to be like this.

- You can help me best by treating me like any other person."

Sam: "There are a number of ways you can help me with my Selective Eating:

- Please try to remember that I've had this all my life – I'm not going to change quickly.

- It would help most if you could stop trying to get me to eat new foods.

- Please don't make fun of my lunchbox just because I have the same foods every day.

- Please do invite me round for a meal, but it would be helpful if you tell your mum and dad what I can't eat.

- Please remember that I do get very worried about eating, especially if there's food on the table I can't eat.

Like Alice, Beth and Freddie:

- Please try to stay friends with me.

- Please try to remember that I like doing lots of things that you do.

- Please try to remember that I haven't chosen to be like this.

- You can help me best by treating me like any other person."

Francesca: "There are a number of ways you can help me with my Functional Dysphagia:

- It would be helpful if you could try to stop making me eat foods I'm afraid of.

- Please don't make fun of me; it's not my fault that I'm afraid.

- Please don't make fun of my lunchbox just because I have the same foods every day.

- Please do invite me round for a meal, but please remember to tell your mum and dad that I can only eat soft foods and that lumpy or solid foods scare me.

- Please remember that I really do believe that I will choke or be sick if I eat solid foods; I know you might think that's silly.

Like the others:

- Please try to stay friends with me.

- Please try to remember that I like doing lots of things that you do.

- Please try to remember that I haven't chosen to be like this.

- You can help me best by treating me like any other person."

"Please remember that we are all normal boys and girls who just happen to have difficulty with our eating. We all sometimes feel sad and worried and still very much want you to be our friends. Please invite us around to your house and to join in at school. Lots of people are trying to help us but we would like you to try and understand how we feel. Thank you!"

How adults can help

If you are worried about a child's eating the best thing you could do to help is to seek professional advice. Please remember that eating disorders affect both boys and girls, of any age and from any culture.

- It's important to remember that we cannot help having our eating disorders.

- We are not to blame and nor are you.

- Eating disorders are like any other illness – they are not chosen or voluntary.

- We would like you to understand that our eating may seem to be the main problem; often we have other worries and upsets too.

- It really isn't helpful if you argue with us, tell us off, get angry with us or pressurise us to eat.

- However, it would be helpful if you could discuss with us what might make eating a bit less difficult.

- Sometimes, just like other people, we feel angry for no obvious reason.

- Remember that our eating disorders are really complicated and that we need professional help in the same way as children with other illnesses do.

Recommended reading, organisations and websites

If you would like to find out more about Eating Disorders, here are some useful books, organisations and websites:

RECOMMENDED READING

Bryant-Waugh, R. and Lask, B. (2013) *Eating Disorders: A Parents Guide*. East Sussex: Routledge.

ORGANISATIONS AND WEBSITES

Beat – beating eating disorders

Wensum House
103 Prince of Wales Road
Norwich
Norfolk
NR1 1DW
Phone: 0300 123 3355
Email: info@b-eat.co.uk
Website: www.b-eat.co.uk

Beat is the UK's leading charity supporting those affected by eating disorders and campaigning on their behalf.

F.E.A.S.T. (Families Empowered & Supporting Treatment of Eating Disorders)
PO Box 11608
Milwaukee, Wisconsin 53211
USA
Email: info@feast-ed.org
Website: http://members.feast-ed.org

F.E.A.S.T is an international organisation supporting families, patients and clinicians working together to treat eating disorders.

National Eating Disorders Association
National Eating Disorders Association
165 West 46th Street
Suite 402
New York, NY 10036
USA
Phone: +1 (212) 575-6200
Email: info@NationalEatingDisorders.org
Website: www.nationaleatingdisorders.org

NEDA is the leading non-profit organisation in the United States advocating on behalf of and supporting individuals and families affected by eating disorders.

Blank for your notes